MUSTANG
An American Classic

Publications International, Ltd.

Louis Weber, CEO
Publications International, Ltd.
7373 North Cicero Avenue
Lincolnwood, Illinois 60712

Manufactured in China.

8 7 6 5 4 3 2 1

ISBN-13: 978-1-4127-1224-8
ISBN-10: 1-4127-1224-6

Library of Congress Control Number: 2005934439

The editors gratefully acknowledge those who supplied photography for this book:

Ford Motor Company; Mitch Frumkin; Chuck Giametta; Bud Juneau; Dave Kutz; Dan Lyons; Vince Manocchi; Doug Mitchel; Mike Mueller; David Newhardt; Rick Popely; Saleen Corporation; Steve Statham; W.C. Waymack; Nicky Wright.

Special thanks to the owners of the cars featured in this book, without whose enthusiastic cooperation this book would not have been possible.

The editors also express their thanks for the generous assistance of the Ford Motor Company.

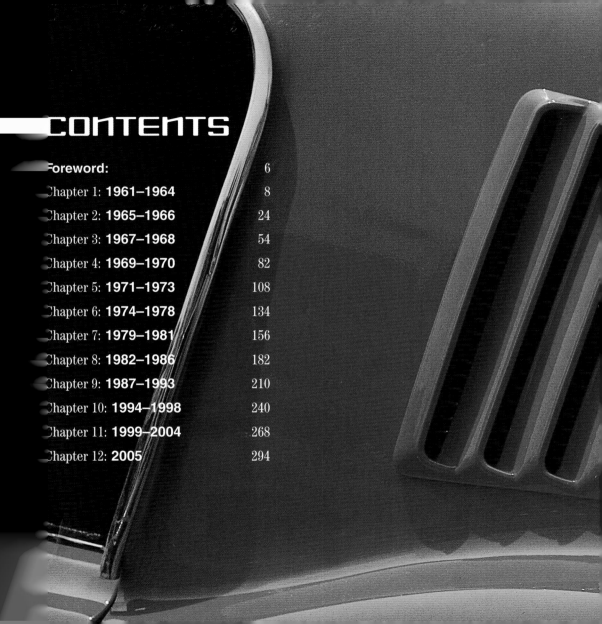

CONTENTS

FOREWORD

It was one of Ford's best ideas: a simple, low-cost small car offering sporty style, a youthful driving spirit, and personal features to suit any taste and budget. Mustang was a huge success from day one, and it's still going strong more than 40 years later.

That's an amazing feat, especially considering how much things have changed since the mid 1960s. The secret? Mustang keeps changing with the times, but its timeless personality doesn't. Mustang has always been about fun and adventure. Always will be. No wonder it's outlived a herd of ponycar imitators—or that it's been so loved by so many for so long.

This book celebrates the iconic breed that keeps galloping into the future at full speed. Enjoy!

CHAPTER 1

1961-1964

Ford's first Mustang was an all-out sports car. Built in 1961, this Mustang I was a small, light two-seater with a race-car-style midengine design. It wowed the press and public alike.

The Mustang I project was supervised by Ford design chief Gene Bordinat (standing) and engineering head Herb Misch (seated). Two cars were built: a "pushmobile" to show the press, and a later running model that the public saw in October 1962. Wheelbase on both was a trim 90 inches.

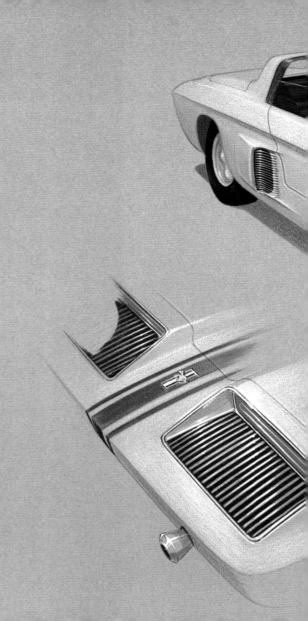

Designers love doodling sports cars, which is how the Mustang I happened.

It was born in a styling studio headed by John Najjar, who rendered these views after his team built a full-size mockup. The later running model lived up to its racy looks by showing great handling, 10 second 0-60-mph scoot, and miserly fuel economy of up to 30 mpg. All this reflected a petite 1500-pound package with an efficient 90-horsepower V-4 engine behind the cockpit.

**Ford Division chief Lee Iacocca vetoed build-
ing the Mustang I for sale.** He thought it was too com-
plex and costly. Iacocca was right, even though the engine and other
components came from Ford parts bins.

Iacocca saw Ford's new sporty car as a youthful, low-cost four-seat job. To get the looks he wanted, he staged a competition among three design teams. Lincoln-Mercury Division sent two cars (right).

6-29-62
S-5529-16

The Mustang styling contest produced hundreds of ideas.

Among the most original were a slew of "Allegros" by the Advanced Design group (far left and bottom). But the winner (left) came from the Ford Division studio headed by Joe Oros. "It was the only one that seemed to be moving," said Lee Iacocca.

Ford suspected its new sporty car would be a sales hit. But just to test the waters one last time, it showed this stylized version, called Mustang II, in fall 1963. Enthusiastic public response convinced Lee Iacocca and other Ford brass that they were on the right track.

Mustang styling went together quickly and was all but finished by October 1963 (above, above right). Even so, cars in some early publicity photos (below) had slightly different trim than regular production models.

Many of the first Mustang ads featured the mainstay hard-top coupe model and its low starting price of just $2368—sensational for a car with such great style. It came with a 101-hp 6-cylinder engine. The sporty long-hood/short-deck stance is evident here.

A snazzy convertible bowed alongside the Mustang hardtop. Both were introduced at the New York World's Fair in April 1964. People loved the new ponycar, and Ford sold 100,000 in just the first four months. Low prices, high value, and a long list of "personal" options made Mustang well-nigh irresistible.

CHAPTER 2

1965-1966

America had never seen a car like Mustang. It was the first American car to combine sports-car styling, low price, and V-8 power. Crowds stampeded some Ford showrooms to get a close look—and to buy. Few suspected that beneath the sporty styling lurked a chassis and powerteams adapted from Ford's humble Falcon compact, a key factor in Mustang's surprising affordability.

M·2587

From the start, Mustang advertising stressed the car's youthful, fun-loving spirit with photos like this one of the rakish convertible. In basic form, the ragtop listed at $2614. That was $246 more than the hardtop coupe, a hefty premium in 1964, so the hardtop always outsold the open-air model.

Mustang was such big news in April 1964 that *Time* and *Newsweek* ran cover stories during the same week. Both cited Ford chief Lee Iacocca as Mustang's father. Another key player was product planner Donald N. Frey, who posed for a publicity photo (above) with Iacocca, the new Mustang, and an earlier Ford megahit, the original 1960 Falcon compact.

Unexpected Price! $2368* f.o.b. Detroit

This low price includes such a generous helping of basic equipment that many people will find nearly all they could ask for in the standard Mustang. Small wonder, because Mustang is so complete it includes many items which come on other cars only at extra cost or not at all.

Room and comfort are basic in Mustang too. It comfortably seats four, or five when you include the children. Doors open extra wide. Front passenger seat-back folds *all the way down* for easy access to the rear. Trunk is surprisingly large, easy to load.

Mustang's dashing body
rested on a simple, rugged chassis.
A thrifty six-cylinder engine was standard, but
buyers could opt for one of two lively, efficient
"small-block" V-8s. Sportier suspension and brakes
were also on Mustang's long options list.

Even a basic Mustang was quite dressy. Full wheel covers and bucket-seat interior were standard. Options could make it downright luxurious. The sporty long-hood/short-deck styling limited cargo room and rear-seat space, but few buyers seemed to mind.

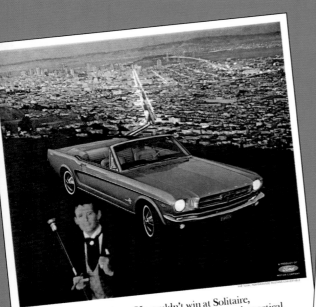

Bernard was a born loser. He couldn't win at Solitaire, even when he cheated. Enter Mustang—the car that's practical, sporty, luxurious. Your choice! Bernard chose the sporty options. Got a 289 cu. in. V-8. Four-on-the-floor. Tachometer and clock combo. Special handling package. Front disc brakes— and did Bernie's luck change!
Yesterday he won San Francisco in a faro game. And now he's got his eye on New York. Mustangers always win.

Best year yet to go Ford
MUSTANG
MUSTANG
MUSTANG

Desmond was afraid to let the cat out...until he got his Mustang. Mustang! A car to make weak men strong, strong men invincible. Mustang! Equipped with bucket seats, floor shift, vin[yl] interior, padded dash, full carpeting, more. Mustang! A challenge[s] your imagination with options like front disc brakes, 4-on-the-flo[or], big 289 cu. in. V-8, you name it. Desmond traded in his Persian kitten for an heiress named Olga. He had to. She followed him home. (It's inevitable...Mustangers have more fun.)

Best year yet to go
MUSTAN
MUSTAN
MUSTAN

Buying a Mustang could change your life. Or so said a series of whimsical first-year ads. To Ford's delight, Mustang appealed to buyers of all ages, hip and square alike.

Wolfgang used to give harpsichord recitals for a few close friends. Then he bought a Mustang. Things looked livelier for Wolfgang, surrounded by bucket seats, vinyl interior, padded dash, wall-to-wall carpeting (all standard Mustang)...and a big V-8 option that produces some of the most powerful notes this side of Beethoven. What happened? Sudden fame! Fortune! The adulation of millions! Being a Mustanger brought out the wolf in Wolfgang. What could it do for you?

Best year yet to go Ford

MUSTANG!
MUSTANG!
MUSTANG!

33

Mustang offered a racy GT option.

It featured bodyside stripes and grille-mounted driving lights. Top available engine was the 271-hp 289-cubic-inch V-8. Many buyers also ordered center shift console and "Rally-Pac" tachometer and clock.

The Five Different Total Performance Cars!

FORD 1965

MUSTANG · FALCON · FAIRLANE · FORD · THUNDERBIRD

Ford expanded the herd for the official 1965 model year with a "2+2" fastback coupe. Several new Mustang options, plus larger base engines, arrived at the same time.

At Ford's request, Carroll Shelby of Cobra sports-car fame created a high-performance Mustang fastback. Called GT-350, it deleted the rear seat to save weight and included a 306-hp V-8.

Mustang was a natural for drag racing. It fast proved a quarter-mile star. Many of the 1965 contestants were much-modified fastbacks like these, sponsored by major Ford dealers. Their many wins helped to confirm Mustang as a true high-performance car.

1966

Ford's ponycar was a runaway success. Detroit hadn't seen anything like it in years. Despite over half a million sales for 1965 and only minor changes for '66, Mustang galloped on, attracting another 608,000 happy buyers in its second model year.

Mustang was barely a yearling in 1966, and Ford saw no need to tamper with its hugely successful formula. Even so, buyers benefited from little-changed prices and several standard-equipment upgrades, including a padded dash and extra gauges.

Oops! Ford staged elaborate publicity shots of the '66 Mustang featuring split-lens taillamps. But Ford axed those taillamps at the last minute to save cost, and returned to the original 1965 style.

**Young or young-at-heart,
everyone loved the Mustang.**

By 1966, the ponycar was established as a
permanent part of the Ford line.

1966

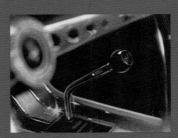

Take a 1966 Mustang convertible. Add the GT package, strong 271-horse 289 V-8, four-on-the-floor transmission, and smart pony interior. *Voilà!* Instant classic.

With the right options, Mustang could be an effective performer on road, track, or dragstrip. The 2+2 fastback was the racer's choice because of its superior high-speed aerodynamics.

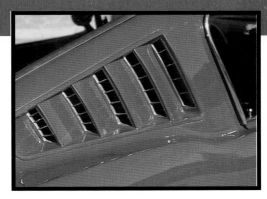

Want to rent a sports car?

Hertz let you do just that, thanks to
Shelby's special GT-350H. Only 936
were built, all for the 1966 model year.

CHAPTER 3

1967-1968

How do you follow a million-seller? Make it even better. Ford did just that with the 1967 Mustang, giving it fresh styling and room for brawny big-block V-8s. A good thing, too, as the ponycar now faced its first real competition in the form of the Chevrolet Camaro.

Mustang looked hotter than ever for 1967, thanks to a lower-body restyle imparting a huskier performance-car look. The update also slightly increased width. This improved handling and allowed offering bulkier big-block V-8 options, starting with a 320-hp 390 cubic-incher.

"Change it—but not too much!" That was Ford's challenge with the 1967 Mustang. Most everyone agreed the result was another winner.

Mustang was hardly out of the gate when Ford began work on the 1967 models. These full-size clay mock-ups from July 1964 are typical of the myriad ideas explored, though most all proposals envisioned a more muscular look. Note here the pumped-up body contours, enlarged tail panel, and smoother, wider rear roof pillars.

Despite their marching orders, Mustang designers let their imaginations run free in the early phases of the '67 effort. They paid particular attention to the fastback, as these work-outs suggest. No styling element seemed sacred. No idea too radical. The main goal was to make the sporty compact look bigger and more grown-up.

11-6-64
S-8033-48

10-20-64
S-7963-9

11-6-64
S-8033-52

The 1967 Mustang was designed to keep the popular ponycar out in front.

Ford knew competitors would show up sooner or later—
as indeed they did for '67.

Ford made fast
work of 1967
Mustang styling,
which was nearly
finished by early
1965.

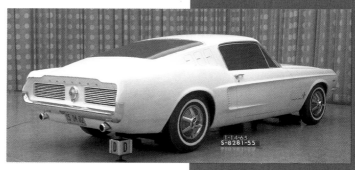

The hardtop remained Mustang's sales mainstay for 1967. It found 356,271 buyers that year. Overall sales dropped 25 percent, however, due to new Chrysler and General Motors competition.

Mustang may have faced imitators for '67, but it outsold them all. More power and new options played a part in that. So did the sharp new looks and many worthwhile underskin improvements.

A sweeping new roofline gave the '67 fastback a genuine high-performance look. It had a base price of $2592. For $200 more, a 320-horse V-8 option provided "go" power to match the fastback's sleek styling.

Also new for '67:
a "shiftable"
automatic trans-
mission and
meaner-looking
Shelby GTs.

Why see a marriage counselor?
Get a Select Shift.

You want a stick shift. *She* wants an automatic. And your budget says: "one car!" No problem anymore. Get *one car*. And get it with a Ford Motor Company Select Shift. The Select Shift is standard equipment with every automatic transmission. Comes on the steering column or on the floor. Works like this: Shift the Select Shift into first or second gear; it works like a *manual shift*. Real control in snow or mud. Assists braking on hills—helps handle heavy trailer loads. Shift the Select Shift into automatic. It's *automatic*. The Select Shift. *You* get your way. *She* gets hers. Ford has a better idea . . . Shift for yourself!

...has a better idea

Ford fired up Mustang's performance image with the 1968 Mach 1 concept.

Based on a stock fastback, it started out wild (bottom photos) and ended up wilder (top photos) by the time it wowed crowds at auto shows. The name and styling were hints of things to come.

Mustang sales fell again for 1968.

A cautious update and still more competition were to
blame. But 300,000 orders was hardly bad, and Ford still
had the number-one-selling ponycar by far.

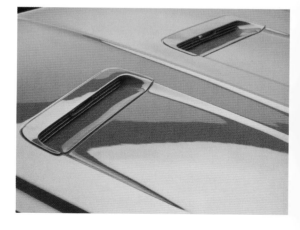

Mustang styling was a bit cleaner for '68. Bodyside "C-stripes" were a racy new hallmark of the desirable GT package option.

America's favorite ponycar was offered in a few special editions for '68. The most popular was the California Special hardtop (above). Available for purchase only in the Golden State, it sold about 5000 copies.

Muscle cars were all the rage in 1968. Mustang kept pace with a potent new V-8 option, the 428-cubic-inch Cobra Jet, with 335 very strong horses.

Mustangs tore up the dragstrips in 1968. Most of those entered in the Super Stock class took advantage of the new Cobra Jet V-8. It came with a ram-air hood scoop, and a street-tuned version could run a quarter-mile in just 13.56 seconds.

Convertibles joined the Shelby-Mustang stable
for 1968. Midyear brought "King of the Road"
G.T. 500s with Cobra Jet V-8s rated at 335 horses,
but actually had closer to 400. Fast? You bet!

The Shelby GT-500 "King of the Road" was the ultimate '68 Mustang.

Identified by its exclusive GT-500KR badging, it boasted the new Cobra Jet engine with ram-air induction. Whether GT-350 or GT-500, the Shelby Mustangs offered awesome performance and aggressive looks for '68.

CHAPTER 4

1969-1970

Mustang was all-new for 1969 looking racier than ever. Overnight, Ford's frisky pony matured into a hot-blooded stallion. Charging out of the gate was the new Mach 1, a performance-oriented fastback packing a 351 V-8 with a strong 250 standard horsepower.

To publicize '69 Mustang performance, new Ford president Semon
E. "Bunkie" Knudsen hired famed drag racer Mickey Thompson and
three other drivers for an assault on Utah's Bonneville Salt Flats. Their
three-car team set nearly 300 speed and endurance records.

The '69 was designed to be a more impressive Mustang in size as well as appearance. The result was a lower, longer, and wider pony with a lot of big-car attitude.

1-7-66
S-9516-8

Styling work for the '69 Mustang was under way by January 1966, as shown by these full-size mockups snapped by Ford photographers. Top brass initially wanted the new design to have the flavor of Ford's posh, personal-luxury Thunderbird.

3-10-66
S9765-10

3-10-66
S9765-6

Designers worked in even more Thunderbird influence during 1966, striving for the massive luxury-car look favored by Lee Iacocca and other top Ford executives. The result included an extended hood, upswept beltline, and a large "loop" grille.

5-23-66
S-10027-22

5-23-66
S-10027-18

Ford took Mustang in two directions for '69, with a new focus on luxury and high performance.

Mustang's signature profile and styling cues were never in doubt for '69, but the final design took over a year to come together. These workouts from mid 1966 show the thinking at about the halfway point.

Mustang went all-out for '69. It offered more models, more power, and more options. Yet buyers didn't have to pay much more. The newly styled and named SportsRoof fastback was a great value, starting at just $2618. And it offered all the style of the hot-rod Mach 1, which carried a $3122 base price.

Taking Mustang luxury to a higher level for '69, the new $2849 Grande hardtop came with vinyl roof covering, wire wheel covers, posh interior trim, and other upscale features.

Performance *and* sophistication?

Mustang options still made it happen in '69. This convertible, for instance, had the available 220-horse 302 V-8 and the Interior Decor Group with wood-grain dash trim.

Unleashed in mid 1969, the Boss 302 looked like a race car—because it was. To reclaim the Trans-Am title from the rival Chevrolet Camaro, Ford created the Boss 302 as a race-ready Mustang that was more than ready for the street. Its heart was a 302-cubic-inch V-8 with close to 400 actual horses.

Besides a "little Boss" for the track, Ford had a "big Boss" for the dragstrip. Another mid-1969 debut, the Boss 429 was humorously rated at 360 horsepower, but in fact was much stronger. Both these Mustangs were virtually custom-built. That's why the Boss 302 sold just 1934 models, the Boss 429 a mere 852.

Left: Carroll Shelby poses with his stable of hot '69 Mustangs. Above: Mustang failed to beat Camaro in the '69 Trans-Am championship, despite the determined efforts of ace drivers like George Follmer.

The sleek 1970 Milano concept alluded to the future of Mustang. Back in the showroom, the 1970 Mustangs offered a freshened update of the all-new '69 design.

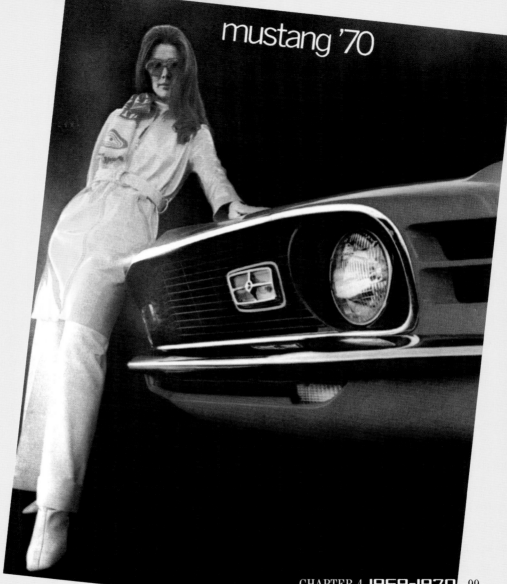

mustang '70

"Mustang's Got Personality!" said the 1970 ads. That it did, yet sales fell for the fourth straight year, sinking below 200,000. The pony-car market had peaked.

100

Ford sweated the details for the 1970.

Mustang styling got special attention, becoming less busy than the '69 look.

The 1970 Mach 1 could be dressed like a Boss 302. Buyers could add features such as a functional spoiler and rear-window slats. Driving lights and ribbed lower-body trim were newly standard, however, and exclusive to this model.

The "Big Boss" 429 sold just 505 models for 1970, then retired. The Boss 302 also made one last stand, but managed higher sales of 6319 units.

The 1970 Shelby-Mustangs were actually unsold '69s.

It was a sign of changing times. They've since become as highly prized as the Boss 302s and 429s.

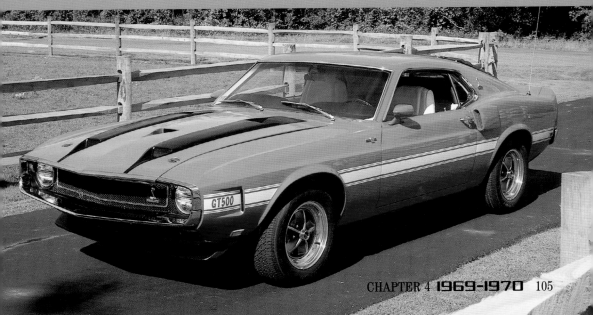

Mustang scored six victories to win the 1970 Trans-Am title.

It was the series' most hard-fought season to date. Besides besting sister Mercury Cougars, Mustang beat out factory-backed Chevrolet Camaros, Pontiac Firebirds, Dodge Challengers, Plymouth Barracudas, and little American Motors' upstart Javelins. This was road racing at its memorable best.

CHAPTER 5

1971-1973

Pony turns Clydesdale! That's how many critics termed the redesigned 1971 Mustangs, the biggest yet. So why were the new ponycars so much larger and heavier? Because Ford had listened to what buyers said they wanted in late 1967, when design work began.

Mustang sounded a patriotic note for 1972 with the red, white, and blue Sprint Decor appearance option. This rakish SportsRoof fastback wears the $347 "B" package, which added mag-style wheels, white-letter tires, and firm suspension to trim features of the $156 "A" group.

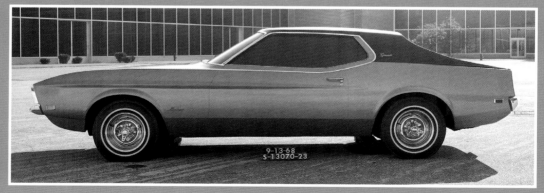

So little time, so much impact. The 1971 Mustang was developed during the brief 19-month Ford presidency of former General Motors exec S.E. "Bunkie" Knudsen. Seeking a more-aggressive hot-car look, Knudsen summarily ordered designers to work from a single basic styling theme that had caught his eye in early 1968.

Knudsen's edict put '71 styling work on a fast track. The new fastback
Mach 1 shown above, for example, was all but done by March 1969.

How big should a ponycar get? Big enough, Ford decided, to provide the extra passenger room that Mustang owners were seeking in the late '60s. The larger package also made room for more flamboyant styling, with a huskier high-performance look.

A near-flat rear roofline marked '71 SportsRoof fastbacks (above left). Hardtops got a swoopy "tunnelback" treatment with inset rear window.

'71 Mustang

Mustang '71 offered more of everything.

Unhappily for performance fans, the big new ponies weighed 500-600 pounds more than the 1969-70 Mustangs. And power was eroded by tighter federal emissions standards. This partly explains why sales kept sliding, down to just under 149,700 for the '71 model year.

Though born to changing times, the 1971 Mustangs changed very little over the next two years. Even so, the jazzy Mach 1 was plenty exciting with the new 429 Cobra Jet V-8 option. The engine packed an alleged 370-375 horsepower, but probably more, in fact.

As before, Mustang offered a variety of wheels and wheel covers for '71. The five-spoke Magnum 500 rims looked great on a Mach 1, which again stood apart from the regular SportsRoof fastback with racy exterior touches like bold body striping and a unique hood.

For Spring Only. A Mustang of a New Stripe.

A New Mustang Hardtop. It's a Special Spring Value at your Ford Dealers. Now.

You take a classic Mustang Hardtop, right? (That practical, comfortable, stylish variety.) Add a sports-car hood—NASA-type scoops and all. Add dual racing mirrors. Color-keyed Spoiler bumper. A unique grille with sport lamps. Brighten the sides with Boss tape stripes. Oh yes, and wide tires with special trim rings. Then take a look at the special prices of the extras. You're home.

Spring won't last forever. Neither will these Special Spring Values at your Ford Dealer's. Now.

Ford

MUSTANG

Mustang options ran the gamut again for '71. Expanding the list in April was a specially priced hardtop (left) sharing many styling features with the macho Mach 1 fastback.

Sporty, personal

MUSTANG '72

...better ideas from Ford

Mustang had little new for '72. Most changes were underneath, and included lower-rated power. Sales dropped to about 125,000 units in a waning overall ponycar market.

MUSTANG GRANDE

MUSTANG HARDTOP

MUSTANG CONVERTIBLE

MUSTANG MACH 1

MUSTANG BOSS 351

MUSTANG SPORTSROOF

Big-block power was gone for '72, but luxury lived on. As before, the easiest route to an uptown Mustang was to order a Grande hardtop. It came with standard vinyl roof cover, extra exterior brightwork, and a posh cabin trimmed in vinyl and "Lambeth" cloth. Priced from $2915 that year, it was a fine sporty-car value.

With Mustang sales flagging in '72, Ford tried some flag-waving. One ploy was the eye-catching Sprint Decor option for fastbacks (below) and hardtops. Ford also built 50 special Sprint convertibles for a Washington, D.C., parade.

The "big hoss" saw little change again for '73, but year-to-year sales climbed for a change. The total was close to 135,000. The Mach 1 (below) sported grille-mounted driving lamps turned from horizontal to vertical.

What makes Mustang different is the way

For eight years now, the Ford Mustang has been the top-selling car in its class.

There are at least three reasons why.

The way it looks.

Sporty, sexy, sleek. You can choose from 5 models: Mach I, SportsRoof, Grandé, Hardtop, and Convertible.

New for 1973, you also get a rugged color-keyed front bumper and a dramatic grille design.

But not all the good looks are on the outside. Inside the

cockpit, you sit back in a bucket seat while your hand drops to a floor-mounted shift console and you look out over a deep-set instrument panel.

The way it handles.

The Mustang's low silhouette and compact size make its handling as beautiful as its looks.

A smoother independent front suspension with anti-sway bar helps take the bumps of rough roads and the twist out of twisting turns.

Giving you d
passenger-car rid

The feeling
a Mustang adds u
do something ver
It's a very di
You can ask
Or you can find o

All 1973 cars must meet Federal Emissions Standards before sale. See your Ford Dealer for details.

ks, handles, and makes you feel.

andling with a comfortable

eels.
ce you get from driving
personal style. Like when you
ctly how you did it.

on people who own a Mustang.
ur Ford Dealer's.

(Some of the fine Mustang options shown on the Grande above are
automatic transmission, air conditioning, AM-FM stereo radio, console, power front
disc brakes, white sidewall tires, and heated backlite. A smart choice too would be
the steel-belted, radial ply tires. Tests show that steel-belted radials can give
average drivers 40,000 miles of tread wear under normal driving conditions.)

FORD MUSTANG

FORD DIVISION

Mustang's success was built on choice. And 1973 was no exception. In fact, no other ponycar offered three body styles, nor as many comfort, convenience, and power options.

**The Mustang rag-
top went on fur-
lough after 1973.**
Ford even gave collectors
a heads-up by announcing
in advance that the ragtop
pony would not be back
for '74. No wonder con-
vertible sales jumped 85
percent to nearly 11,900
for the model year. A
memorable era was over.

CHAPTER 6

1974-1978

Mustang II was a fresh start for Ford's pony-car. Timely, too. Arriving almost simultaneously with an unprecedented gas shortage, it was smaller than even the original Mustang, with economy-car fuel thrift perfect for the times. Mustang II was also a "little jewel," with much-improved quality and a high level of standard equipment. Lee Iacocca said his new baby would "turn the small-car market on its ear." And in a way, it did.

How small should a ponycar be? At first, Ford wanted to do another monster 'Stang (right, opposite page upper left). Instead, it opted to go after popular sporty import coupes led by the Toyota Celica and Ford's own German Capri.

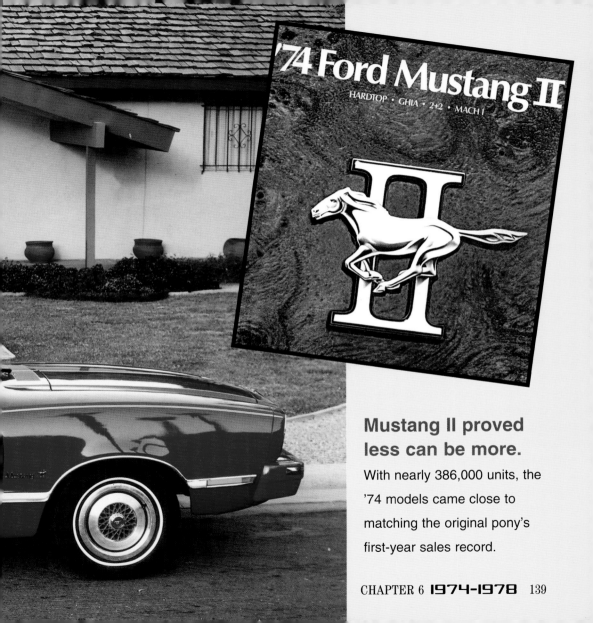

Mustang II proved less can be more.

With nearly 386,000 units, the '74 models came close to matching the original pony's first-year sales record.

140

"A new class of small car: First Class." That's how Ford touted the Mustang II. Backing up the brag were many new Mustang features, plus notchback and new hatchback coupe styles which Ford termed a "right size" package. The new Mach 1 hatchback (top, far right) used a lively V-6 that was optional for other models in lieu of a thrifty four-cylinder. Standard floorshift? Of course.

1975
Ford Mustang II

Our small, sporty personal car

Mustang II Ghia with Silver Luxury Group

Hardtop • Ghia • 2+2 • Mach 1

The closer you look, the better we look.

142

Rather have a V-8? Ford obliged by reviving its 302-cubic-inch small-block engine as an option for 1975 Mustang IIs. New dress-up options gave the Ghia hardtop the look and feel of a traditional big luxury liner.

Mustang II was speedy in spirit, if not in fact.

Though fast cars were all but legislated out of existence by 1976, Mustang IIs could still have a "hot-car" look if ordered with that year's new Stallion trim or Cobra II package.

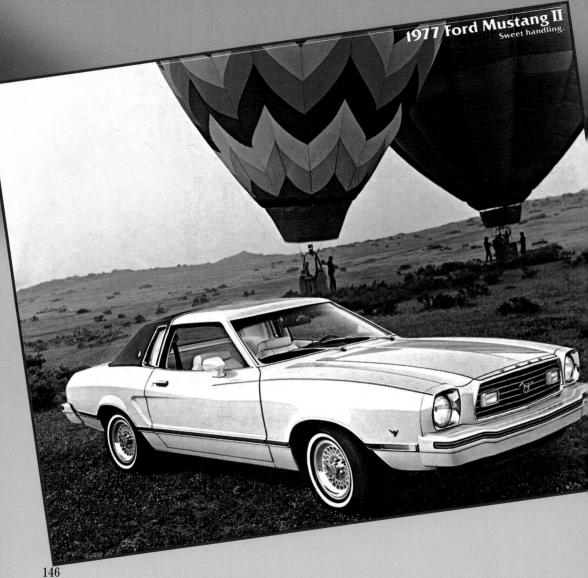

1977 Ford Mustang II
Sweet handling.

Despite few changes, Mustang II was popular for five full years. Annual Mustang sales after 1974 reached 180,000 units or more, except for 1977, which drew some 150,000 orders. Yet even '77 sales outpaced the big 1971-73 models. Ford kept buyers interested with new options each year, such as a trunklid luggage rack for '77 hardtops.

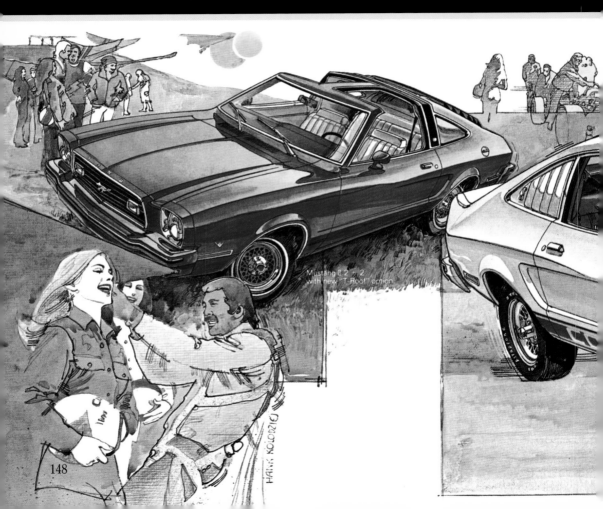

Looking for fun? Mustang II had it. Fresh-air fiends applauded the new T-bar roof option for '77 fastbacks. Just lift off the twin panels above the cockpit and *voilà*! Instant convertible.

Mustang II 2 + 2 with new "T-Roof" option

HANK KOLODZIEJ

A fine handler with its firm suspension, the racy Cobra II package returned for '77 with more color schemes, including red stripes over white paint.

Mustang II Cobra II

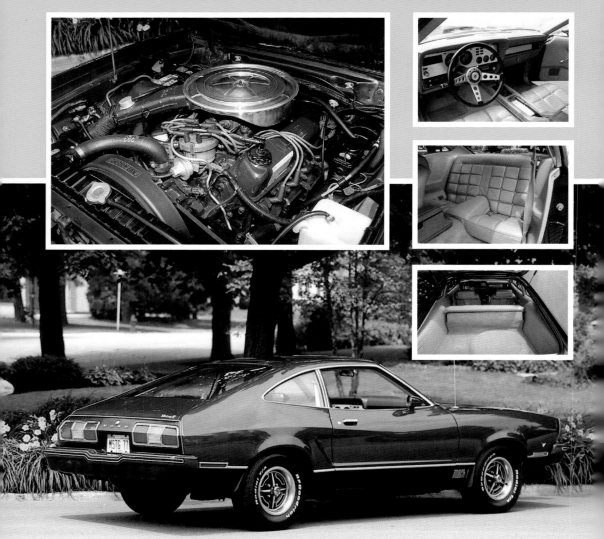

Let's get personal. Like earlier Mustangs, the II offered options to suit most any taste and budget: V-8, sunroof, 8-track tape player, interior upgrades, and more.

Great pretender? With the V-8 and other options, the Mustang II was a good performer for its day. Actually, no Detroit car could offer blazing '60s-style speed by the late 1970s.

Hail the King: King Cobra, that is. New for '78, Mustang II's final year, this option went beyond the Cobra II with a standard V-8, uprated chassis, and even wilder styling.

154

CHAPTER 7

1979-1981

Mustang was reborn with the "New Breed" of 1979. Combining the best of American and European thinking, this all-new design took the ponycar concept back to its roots. It was an efficient, affordable fun machine with trendsetting style, but also thoroughly modern engineering and performance. Americans loved it, snapping up 370,000 Mustangs for '79. Though sales would later seesaw, this basic design was so "right" that it would carry on for no less than 14 years. No wonder these Mustangs still have legions of fans.

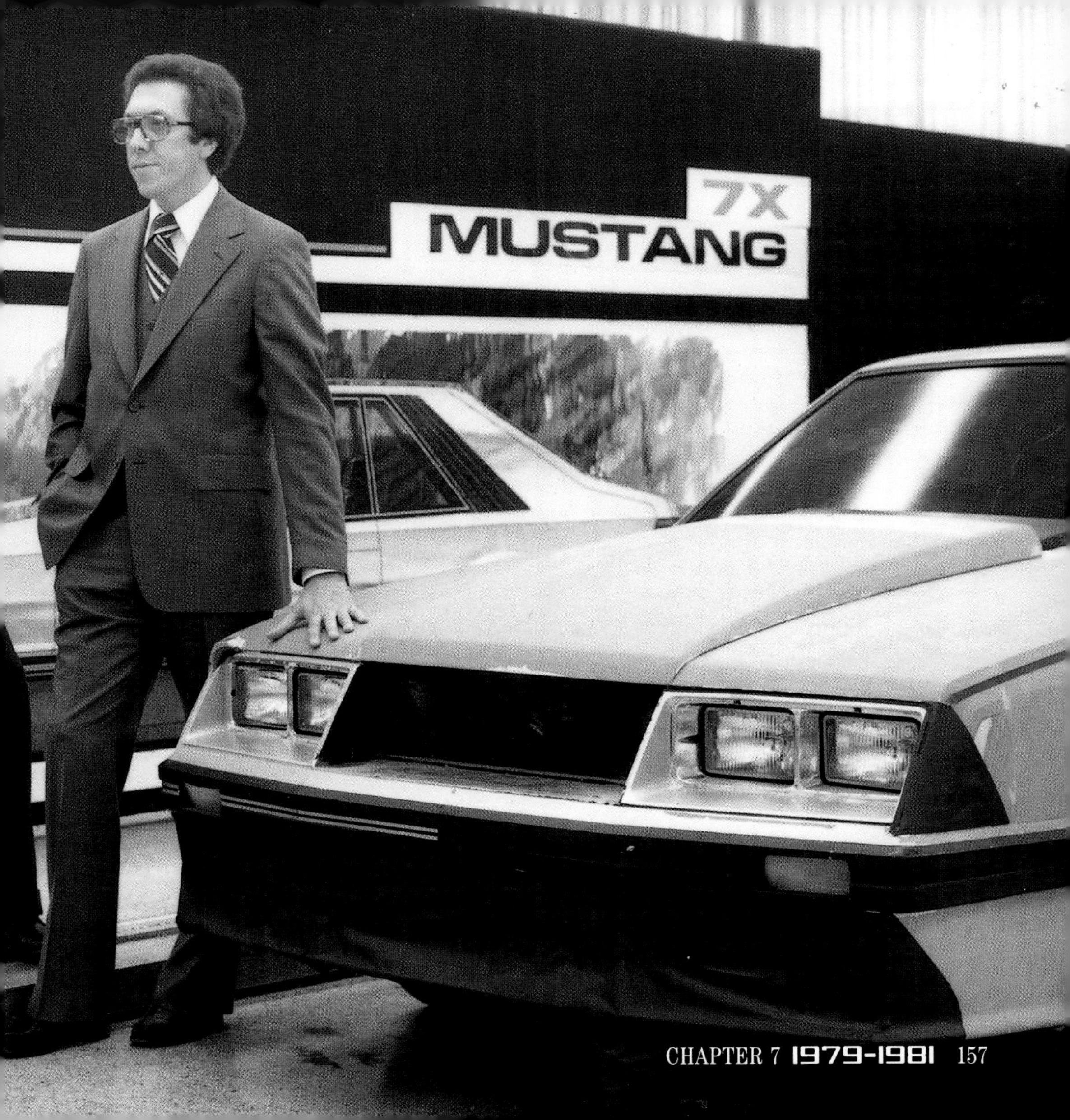
7X
MUSTANG

The '79 Mustang showed plenty of European flair. Chief program designer Jack Telnack had worked in Europe, and Ford's Ghia studio in Italy submitted proposals to compete with Ford's own stylists in Dearborn. Here, a sample of early workouts from 1974-76.

Clean, trim, slick.

Those were the goals for
'79 Mustang styling. Ford
designers took special
pains to create a shape
with minimal air drag, an
important factor in Detroit's
new quest to increase fuel
economy. The '79 Mustang
was based on another
Ford compact, the new-
for-'78 Fairmont. But a
generous budget allowed
using many specific underskin components so looks
and performance would
not be compromised.

1979 FORD
MUSTANG
A whole new breed.

16

Notchback or hatch-back? Mustang again offered both for '79. Plus an intriguing new turbocharged four-cyl engine, a nonturbo four, V-6, and veteran 302-cubic-inch V-8. There were also three suspension setups and the usual plethora of optional features. Base prices were up to around $4000, but that was quite attractive at the time.

At home on road *and* track. Mustang was 1979's Indy 500 pace car. Ford sold some 11,000 replicas. Hatchbacks also offered a sporty new Cobra performance package for '79 (right).

More of a good thing for 1980.

Though little changed for its sophomore season, the "New Breed" added a Carriage Roof option for notchback coupes that simulated the top-up look of a convertible.

Mustang 2-Door with Sport Option

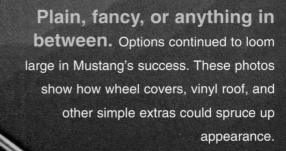

Plain, fancy, or anything in between. Options continued to loom large in Mustang's success. These photos show how wheel covers, vinyl roof, and other simple extras could spruce up appearance.

Mustang 3-Door Cobra

Pace car looks, pace and handling for the street.

The 1980 Cobra package picked up styling cues from the '79 pace car. A special suspension with Michelin tires and tri-spoke wheels again delivered trackworthy handling. The punchy turbo-four could deliver 0-60 mph in 11-12 seconds—hot stuff by standards of the day.

Take a seat, any seat.

They're all good. This group of catalog photography highlights the many interior trim options listed for 1980 Mustangs. They were enough to make your head spin: cloth, cloth and vinyl, and all vinyl in numerous colors and patterns. A "mini" center console was standard, but a longer version with center armrest and storage compartments was available. Enthusiasts loved the no-nonsense dashboard with standard full instrumentation and convenient European-style stalk controls for lights and wipers.

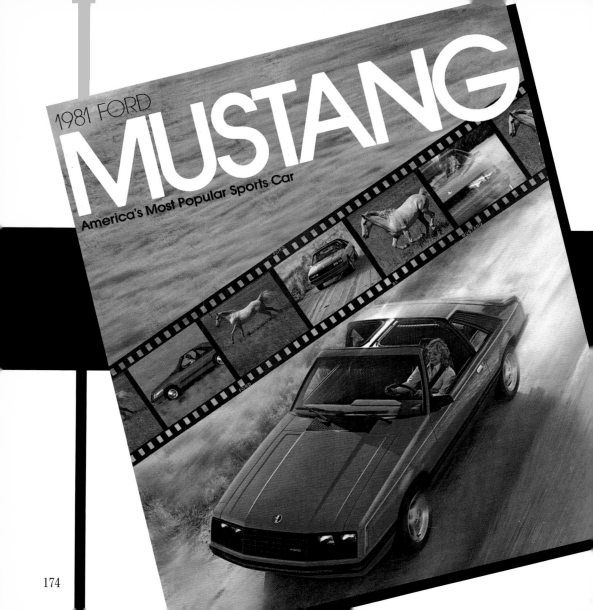

1981 FORD

MUSTANG

America's Most Popular Sports Car

Raise the roof—or not. An optional twin-panel T-top roof returned for 1981 Mustangs. The available "Carriage Roof" continued for notchbacks (below), which also looked good without.

Dressed for success. "New Breed" styling still looked good, even in original form. Most every critic deemed it more tasteful and exciting than the Mustang II design.

Thrills with thrift.

Properly equipped, Mustang could deliver what a 1981 ad promised. A tilt/takeout glass sun-roof was an open-air option to the T-top treatment.

Suddenly, you're at the wheel of America's most popular sports car. Suddenly, the moment is Mustang. Driving is a new sensation. Finely tuned excitement. Precision handling. Suddenly, it's Mustang. Hot stuff.

FORD MUSTANG
FORD DIVISION *Ford*

Hot Stuff

Must

TURN HIGH MILEAGE INTO HI

34 EST HWY. (23) EPA EST MPG. Estimates for comparison. Your mileage may differ, depending on speed, distance and weather. Actual highway mileage and Calif. estimates lower.

ng.

CITEMENT.

GOOD/YEAR POLYSTEEL RADIAL

The '81 Mustang Lineup

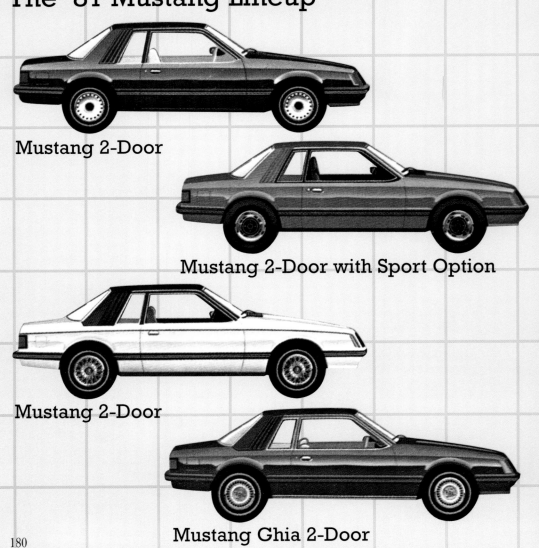

Mustang 2-Door

Mustang 2-Door with Sport Option

Mustang 2-Door

Mustang Ghia 2-Door

Mustang 3-Door

Mustang Cobra 3-Door

Mustang Ghia 3-Door

CHAPTER 8

1982-1986

Mustang thrived anew in the '80s.

Model-year sales reached an all-time low in 1983, at under 120,900 units. But sales grew as Ford kept turning up the heat on styling and performance. A special confection for 20th-anniversary 1984 was a GT-350 convertible done up in Oxford White and Canyon Red.

New bosses and a new Boss.

Enthusiastic new managers took command in 1980. They soon OK'd a hotter V-8 for a reborn Mustang GT. These work-outs are close to what appeared for 1982. Other models (top right) got minor styling updates.

Hop it up, drop the top. The GT (right) returned as a uniquely styled hatchback with 157 horses and lots of fast-car features for $8308. The price-leader L coupe (top) started at $6345 for '82. A convertible was promised for model year 1983.

A dash of distinction. All 1982 Mustangs used the same basic instrument-panel design that had been around since 1979. And that was fine, because it remained one of Detroit's best—very "European" in look and function. Pseudo-wood accents were included with the luxury-focused, top-level trim packages.

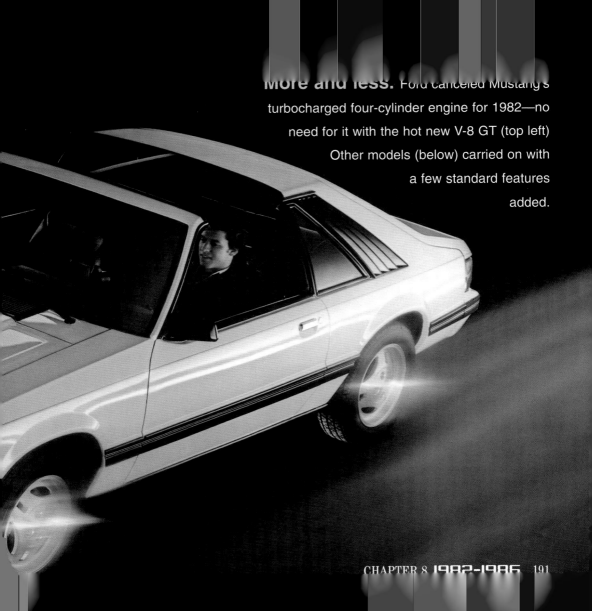

More and less. Ford canceled Mustang's turbocharged four-cylinder engine for 1982—no need for it with the hot new V-8 GT (top left) Other models (below) carried on with a few standard features added.

1983 FORD MUSTANG

Put on an "aero" face. A smooth new nose helped 1983 models get slightly better fuel economy— including Mustang's first convertible in a decade.

192

Full Gallop. The '83 GT (top right) boasted 175 horses for '83. Other models got more improvements. Mustang was back racing by now, and fast piling up the wins.

1984 Ford Mustang

A steed for every need. A 165-hp V-8 was a new option for non-GT 1984 models (below). Buyers could also opt for a Turbo GT package—but few did. Back from '83, it had a "blown" 145-hp four-cylinder.

Horse of a different color. One of 1984's major surprises was the European-inspired SVO hatchback. Besides unique styling and a much-modified chassis, it boasted a hot turbo-four engine with 175 horses. The SVO was good for 0-60 mph in 7.5 seconds.

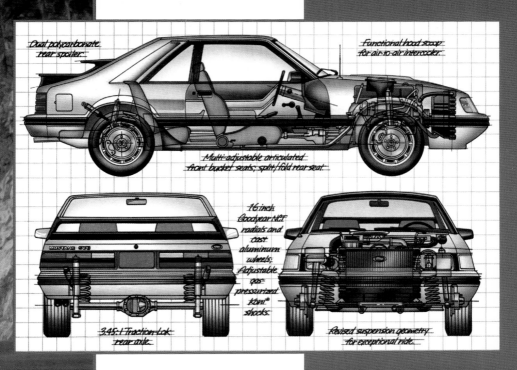

Dual polycarbonate
rear spoiler.

Functional hood scoop
for air-to-air intercooler.

Multi-adjustable articulated
front bucket seats; split/fold rear seat.

16-inch
Goodyear NCT
radials and
cast
aluminum
wheels.
Adjustable
gas-
pressurized
Koni®
shocks.

3.45:1 Traction-Lok
rear axle.

Raised suspension geometry
for exceptional ride.

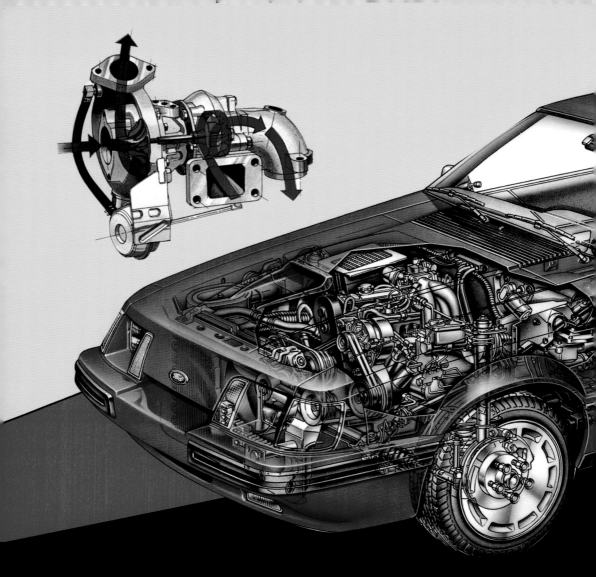

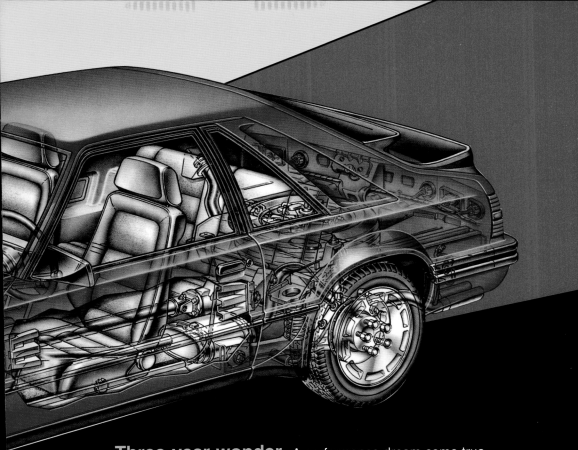

Three-year wonder. A performance dream come true, the SVO offered sophisticated styling and loads of hi-tech engineering. But most Mustangers preferred V-8 GTs, which were just as quick, for thousands less. As a result, Ford gave up on the SVO after 1986 and total output of just 9844 units.

Not new, but further improved. All Mustangs got another nose job and more detail changes for 1985. Additional V-8 tweaking swelled GT horsepower to 210 maximum. It boosted sales, too.

Sophisticated screamer. Flush headlamps marked 1985-86 SVOs, which also added 30 horses for 210 total. These rare Fords are now coveted collector cars.

Winning formula. Despite higher prices, Mustang sales surged to nearly 224,500 for 1986, when all GTs got a more-efficient 200-horse V-8.

Plain or fancy? By 1986, you could have "5.0" V-8 muscle in a flashy GT or with quieter base-model styling (below). Either way, you had to beware of the equally fast Pursuit Package Mustangs that were being used by many state highway-patrol units.

CHAPTER 9

1987-1993

By 1987, Mustang was outselling its General Motors' rivals—*combined*.

As if to celebrate, Ford gave it a full makeover, with fresh styling and more power. Oddly, sales stumbled to some 159,000 units, but rebounded to over 211,000 for 1988.

Mustang's 1987 redesign was prompted by rising sales. But there were also outcries from Mustang fans over a rumored Ford plan to replace the V-8 rear-wheel-drive ponycar with a front-drive V-6 design from Japanese affiliate, Mazda. Fortunately, for all concerned, Ford released that car with another name. The beloved Mustang got a new lease on life. Ford marked Mustang's 25th anniversary in model year 1989 with more "then and now" PR photos like this.

You *can* teach an old ponycar new tricks. The 1987 Mustangs proved it. Especially GTs, which got an aggressive new look in line with Ford's corporate "aero" styling theme. These views of the GT convertible spotlight the "grille-less" nose and "cheese-grater" taillights adopted as part of the stem-to-stern restyle.

More power? No problem. The veteran 302-cubic-inch, 5.0-liter small-block V-8 gained 25 horses for '87—a total of 225. Standard for GTs (left) and LX 5.0 models, the V-8 was so popular that supplies ran short during the 1987 run.

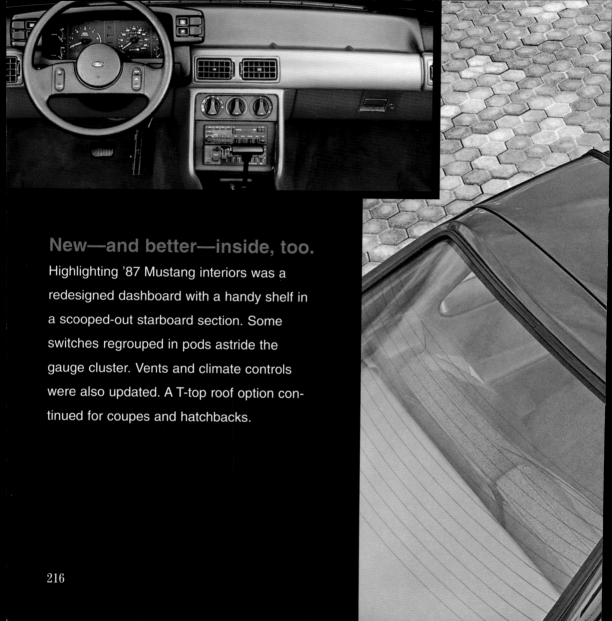

New—and better—inside, too.

Highlighting '87 Mustang interiors was a
redesigned dashboard with a handy shelf in
a scooped-out starboard section. Some
switches regrouped in pods astride the
gauge cluster. Vents and climate controls
were also updated. A T-top roof option continued for coupes and hatchbacks.

You want a V-8 with that? The mainstream LX coupe, hatchback, and convertible returned for 1988 with quieter styling than GTs. A V-8 package—with stealthy "5.0" front-fender ID—was an $1885 option to the thrifty 2.3-liter base four-cylinder.

A birthday, but no presents.

Mustang was again little-changed for 1989, but Ford celebrated the ponycar's 25th birthday with two big bashes and a few smaller events. Sales eased to just below 210,000.

The Saleen solution.

Southern California's Steve Saleen
began building custom-tuned Mustangs
in 1984. His business thrived. For 1989,
he offered these hot SSC models with
292 horses.

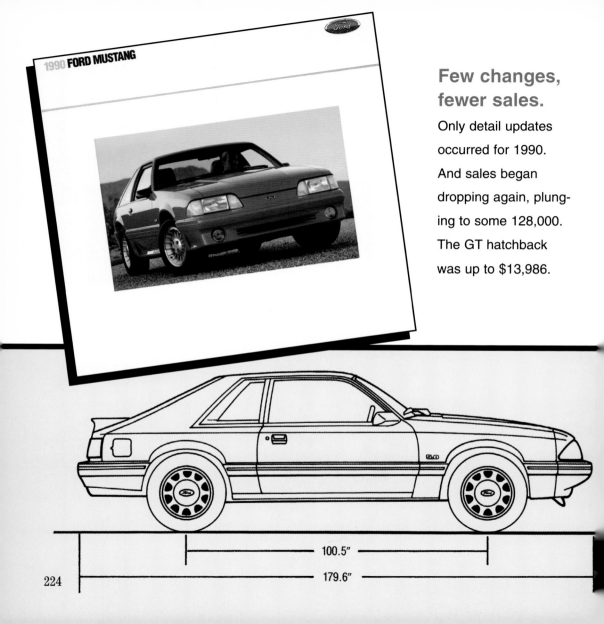

Few changes, fewer sales.

Only detail updates occurred for 1990. And sales began dropping again, plunging to some 128,000. The GT hatchback was up to $13,986.

100.5"

179.6"

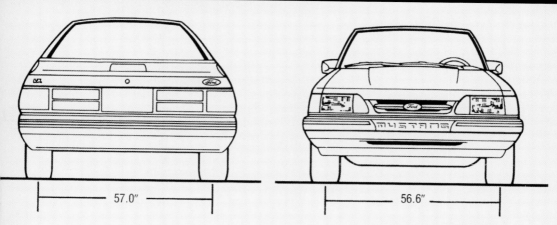

57.0"

56.6"

Hide inside. Among Mustang's few alterations for 1990 was the addition of leather interior trim as a $489 option. That year's LX 5.0 hatchback (below) started at $13,007, its coupe sister at $12,164.

Air on the side of safety. All 1990 Mustangs got a standard driver-side airbag to meet new federal rules for passive restraints. Hidden in the steering wheel, it was rigged to inflate automatically during a crash.

Mustang was a hobbled horse for 1991. Though Mustang remained a terrific performance buy, sales in '91 plunged to 98,737 as a sharp recession took hold. Changes were again few, but V-8 models picked up handsome new five-spoke wheels.

Fast, fair-weather fun. A lower-profile "top stack" improved convertible appearance for 1991, as shown on these LX ragtops. V-8 sales had been steadily growing and were now twice those of four-cylinder models, split evenly between GTs and LX 5.0s.

Hold on. Mustang sales hit an all-time low 79,280 for 1992, yet another year of little news. But racy Mach III show car (opposite page, bottom) hinted that big changes were coming.

So long, old paint. Mustang's basic 1979 styling took a final bow for 1993. Despite all-new GM competition that model year, sales bounced back to over 114,000. A six-model lineup continued (above). New Feature Package options in yellow and white included color-keyed windshield frames.

Snake attack!

Ford unleashed a hot new 235-hp Cobra hatchback for 1993, but built just 5000. A stripped, track-only R version (opposite page, bottom) saw a mere 107 copies.

CHAPTER 10

1994–1998

"It Is What It Was," said ads for the rejuvenated 1994 Mustang. Actually, it almost wasn't. In fact, Ford was about to retire the old warhorse. But it heard that General Motors was planning all-new ponycars of its own. With that, plus input from consumer "gallop polls," Ford gave Mustang's vintage-'79 Fox platform an extreme makeover. It gained modern chassis and powertrain engineering, topped with 60's-inspired retro styling. It was a great way to start Mustang's second 30 years, and sales galloped ahead.

240

Future indicative.

Known within Ford as SN95, the 1994 Mustang was previewed by the '92 Mach III concept, posing left with future CEO William C. Ford, Jr. (left) and his executive cousin, Edsel B. Ford II. Design work began in 1989, and aimed to reinterpret the youthful look of early Mustangs for a new generation of sporty-car buyers.

Wild, mild, just right. Execs debated three SN95 finalist designs dubbed "Rambo," "Bruce Jenner," and "Arnold Schwarzenegger" (above, from left). The last was chosen as the basis for 1994 styling.

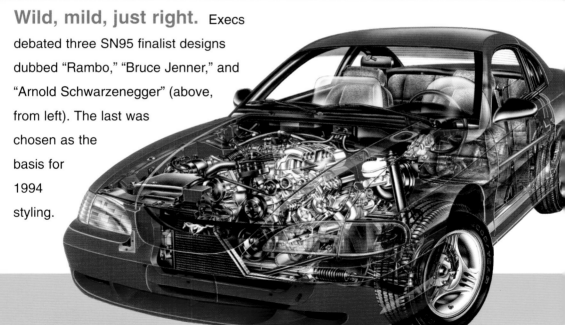

Keeping it simple. The 1994 Mustang bowed in V-6 base trim and in V-8 GT form. Both offered convertible and nonhatchback-coupe body styles. Power was up to 145 horses for base models and to 215 for V-8s. Prices started at an attractive $13,365.

The same, but better. The extensive 1994 redesign produced a slightly larger Mustang with suspension layout and floorpan the only major carryover components. The interior remained classic four-seater with a snug aft cabin, but SN95 had a much stronger structure and visibly improved workmanship.

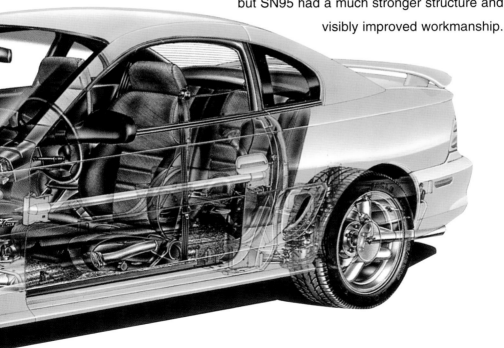

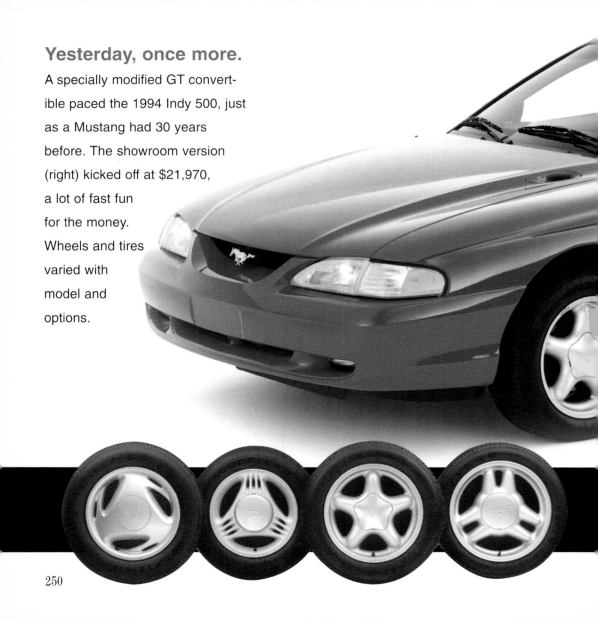

Yesterday, once more.

A specially modified GT convertible paced the 1994 Indy 500, just as a Mustang had 30 years before. The showroom version (right) kicked off at $21,970, a lot of fast fun for the money. Wheels and tires varied with model and options.

1995 FORD

MUSTANG

Back to the future, back to the track.
Though little changed for '95, the SN95 Mustang was already a power in road-racing. Jack Roush's team won the 1994 Trans-Am manufacturer's Cup for Ford.

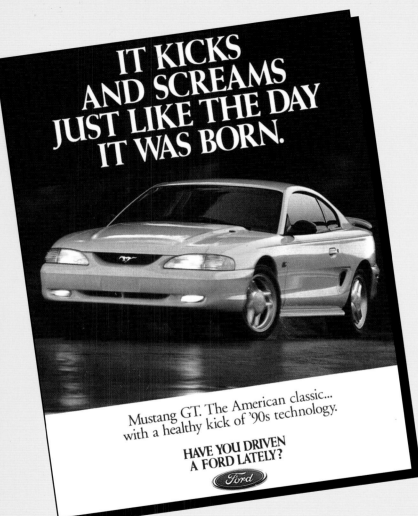

IT KICKS AND SCREAMS JUST LIKE THE DAY IT WAS BORN.

Mustang GT. The American classic... with a healthy kick of '90s technology.

HAVE YOU DRIVEN A FORD LATELY?

The good *new* days. After moving past 123,000 units for '94, Mustang sales hit nearly 186,00 for 1995, despite few changes. Ford ads in this period played the nostalgia card, highlighting the car's growing string of racing victories.

GTs were usually shown, but V-6 base models accounted for most sales. Coupes always outpolled convertibles. Mustang also offered hotter SVT Cobra versions in 1994-95 with 235 horses, special suspension, and unique trim features.

Ford Mustang GT

The fastest ponies always come from race horses.

Before you get a new Ford Mustang GT, consider a background check. Because every street Mustang has racing in its fuel lines. Not to mention other components like engines, transmissions and brakes. Because we test our technology on the world's most challenging race courses. Then we put these advanced new ideas into the Ford you can drive. It's our theory of evolution.

HAVE YOU DRIVEN A FORD LATELY? Ford

Performance 'R Us. Though GM rivals had more stock horsepower than early SN95s, Ford dealers offered a slew of hop-up equipment to close the gap. The SVT group went one better for 1995, with a new 300-hp 351-cubic-inch V-8 Cobra R coupe. Just 250 were built—but for racing only.

Tech talk. The big change for 1996 was a hi-tech, overhead-cam V-8 for GTs. Though the new 4.6-liter made no more power than the veteran 5.0-liter it replaced, most critics judged it an improvement. And performance was no less exciting, with 0-60-mph sprints a swift 6.6 seconds. Even so, model-year sales fell to 135,620.

Mustang

America's original fun-to-drive sports car with new high-tech V-8 power

▲ *Mustang GT Convertible in Crystal White Clearcoat.*

◀ *Far left: The Mustang GT in Deep Violet Clearcoat Metallic.*

◀ *The Mustang GT interior in Black.*

Some equipment shown on these pages may be optional.

FORD MUSTANG

Engine
3.8L OHV V-6 with sequential multiple-port EFI; GT: 4.6L V-8 with sequential multiple-port EFI

Transmission
5-speed manual overdrive (electronic 4-speed automatic overdrive optional)

Front Suspension
Modified MacPherson strut-type, stabilizer tube, nitrogen gas-pressurized hydraulic shocks; GT: Handling components

Rear Suspension
4-bar link coil spring system, stabilizer tube, nitrogen gas-pressurized hydraulic shocks; GT: Handling components plus horizontal-mounted axle dampers

Steering
Power rack-and-pinion

Brakes
Power 4-wheel disc; anti-lock brake system optional

Safety
Driver and front passenger air bag supplemental restraint system; 3-point lap/shoulder belts front and rear

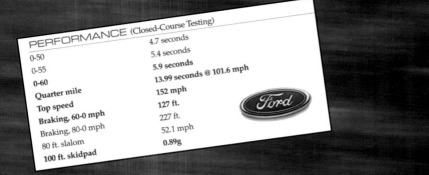

PERFORMANCE (Closed-Course Testing)	
0-50	4.7 seconds
0-55	5.4 seconds
0-60	5.9 seconds
Quarter mile	13.99 seconds @ 101.6 mph
Top speed	152 mph
Braking, 60-0 mph	127 ft.
Braking, 80-0 mph	227 ft.
80 ft. slalom	52.1 mph
100 ft. skidpad	0.89g

Speedier snake. A special twincam version of the new GT V-8 took the SVT Cobra coupe and convertible to 305 horses for 1996, thus finally ending the power gap with top GM rivals. Performance matched Ford claims, which may be why Cobra sales almost doubled to just over 10,000 units.

Three-peat Tommy.

Tommy Kendall won the Trans-Am driver's title in 1995-97 with Roush Racing Mustangs. He also took the 1995 24 Hours of Daytona, co-driving with ace Mark Martin and an actor fellow by the name of Paul Newman.

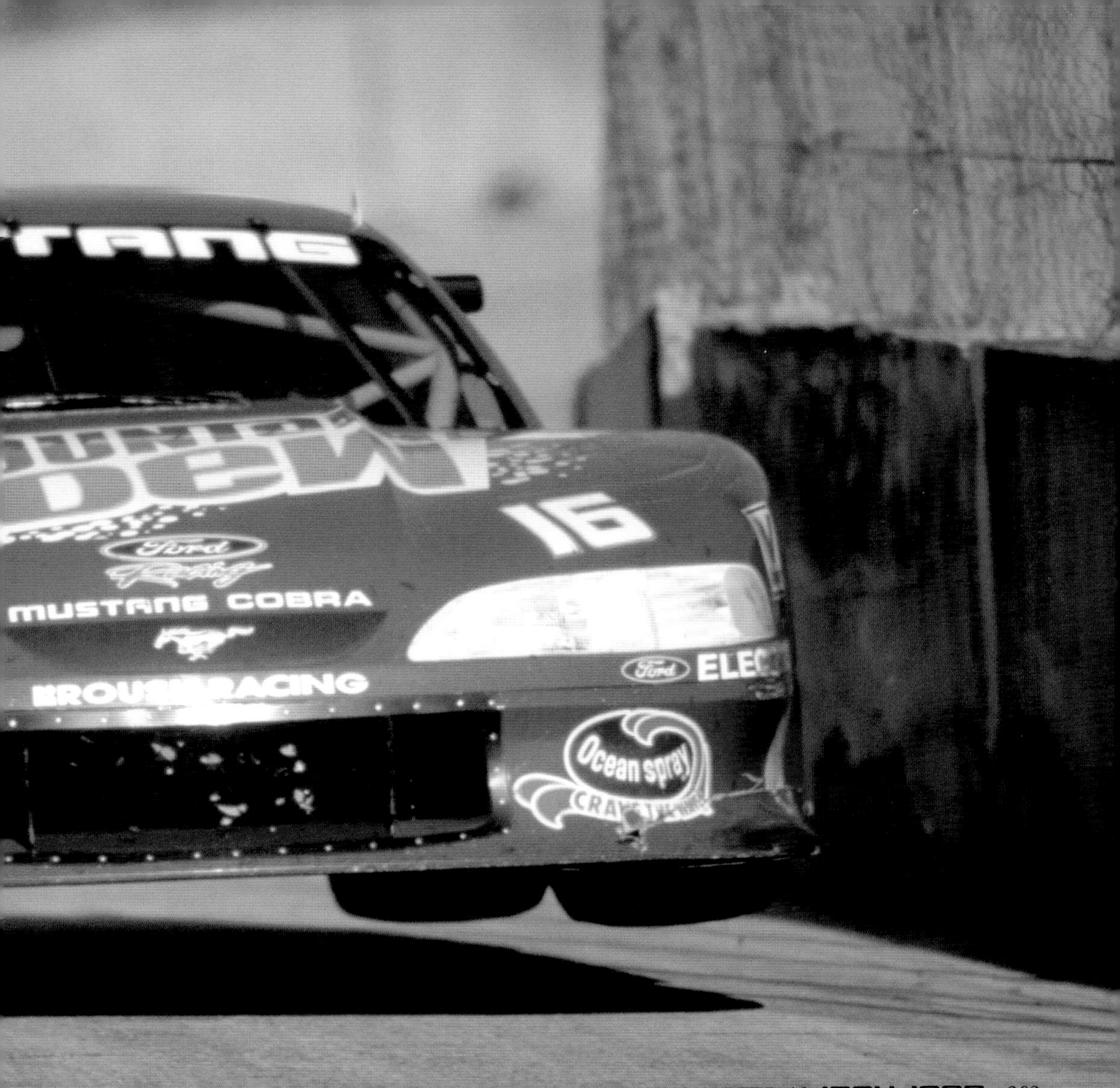
16
MUSTANG COBRA
Ocean spray

Ford Motorsport SVO
PERFORMANCE EQUIPMENT

How Do You Build A Legend?

Mustang with Cobra "R" Hood, Cobra "R" Wheels and new SVO Side Exhaust

When it comes to building a Mustang Cobra "R" replica, all it takes is these parts from Ford Motorsport SVO. These are the exact parts, made by the same OEMs, that made the original SVT Mustang Cobra "R" an instant success. And they're ... you need to give your 1994-1996 Mustang the same legendary looks and performance.

OTHER COBRA "R" PARTS AVAILABLE FROM FORD SVO

- Cobra "R" Hood M-16612-R58 (Pictured)
- Cobra "R" Master Cylinder M-2032-R58*
- Clutch Housing M-6392-R58*
- Line Oil Cooler M-6642-R58*
- 351 HO SVO Engine M-6007-A351*
- Cobra "R" Brake Kit M-2300-K
- Aluminum Radiator M-8005-R58*
- "De-Gas" Bottle M-8080-R58*

The Mustang Cobra "R" front fascia is available through your local Ford Dealer.

To order your Ford Motorsport Equipment catalog, send $5.00 in U.S. funds to:

Ford Motor Company
Dept. MM
P.O. Box 51394
Livonia, MI 48151

*Not legal for sale or use on pollution-controlled motor vehicles.
**Direct replacement part.

Technical "Hot Line"
(810) 468-1356

Mustang Wheel
M-1007-R58**

Koni Front Struts
M-18124-R58
Koni Rear Shocks
M-18125-R58

1994-96
Mustang Cat
Back Side
Exhaust Kit
M-5200-MJ

Tremec 5-Speed
H.D. Transmission
M-7003-R58**

Front Springs M-5310-R58
Rear Springs M-5560-R58

351W Shorty Headers
M-9430-R58**

Jack had the monster (aka: Mustang GT) at the world's longest red light.

And he was putting every watt in that MACH 460 sound system to very good use. That's when

an eager trooper, sitting in his squad car. Waiting. Their eyes met .

The trooper's hand twitched over his holstered radar gun. When the light final...

Just so Smokey could take one last, long look. After all, why try to inspire "fear"...

4.6-LITER SEFI V-8

4-WHEEL DISC BRAKES WITH AVAILABLE ABS

17" WHEELS WITH 245/45ZR17 TIRES*

ROCKIN' 460-WATT SOUND SYSTEM*

*Optional equipment

Steroid therapy. Ford kept pushing over-the-counter performance for 1997 through its Motorsport division, whose catalog was a speed freak's

264

...k eased the monster's V-8 into "slow cruise,"

...en "envy" is perfectly legal?

Built Ford to Last

Mustang GT

1-800-258-FORD or www.ford.com

Ford Motorsport SVO
PERFORMANCE EQUIPMENT

Proven power and performance

...hen it comes ...powering up ...ustangs for peak ...formance, Ford ...O's track record ...aks for itself.

...GT-40 "Street ...." parts were ...st high per- ...nce parts on ...rket for the ...g 5.0.

...ecause ...arts are ...d and ...tured by Ford Motor Company and select ...iers to meet our stringent quality standards.

...ading racers like Steeda Auto Sports and ...ing rely on SVO performance parts to get their ...Mustang 5.0L engines ready to race and win.

So why settle for less with your Mustang 5.0L? Satisfy your need for high perfor- mance with the same proven parts the professionals trust – GT-40 "Street Legal" parts from Ford Motorsport SVO.

50 States Street Legal

GT–40 "Street Legal" parts from Ford Motorsport SVO

- Dyno tested at 270 Horsepower
- Meets emission requirements of regular production 5.0L Mustang engines
- Available only for 1982–1995 models with mass-air electronic fuel injection and T-5 manual transmission

65mm Throttle Body
M-9926-A302

Roller Rocker Arm
(1.60:1 ratio)
M-6564-B351

Shorty Headers
(Stainless Steel)
M-9430-SSC
M-9430-C50

Throttle Body EGR Spacer
M-9474-A50

GT-40 EFI Upper
Intake Manifold
M-9424-A51

EFI Electric Fuel Pump
M-9407-A50

GT-40 Cylinder Heads
M-6049-Y302

T-5 Manual Transmission
M-7003-Z

Serpentine Belt Horsepower
Pulley Kit
M-8509-A50

GT-40 EFI Lower
Intake Manifold
M-9461-A50

**Technical "Hot Line"
(810) 468-1356**

To order your Ford Motorsport Equipment catalog, send $5.00 in U.S. funds to:

Ford Motor Company
Dept. 5.0
P.O. Box 51394
Livonia, MI 48151

---

dream book. Just as well, as Mustangs changed little that year. Even so, ads still stressed the stock GT's high bang-for-buck quotient.

End of a line. Mustang's basic '94 styling took a final bow for 1998. GTs muscled up to 225 horses. Changes were few otherwise, but sales jumped to 175,522. SVT Cobras were still limited to 10,000, but sold out for the second year in a row.

CHAPTER 11
1999-2004

Let's party, 'cause it's 1999! Ford did just that for Mustang's 35th-birthday year, despite red ink on the balance sheet and turmoil in the executive suite. With fresh styling, more power, and appreciated new features for '99, Mustang was in its best shape in many a year. No wonder tens of thousands of Mustangers gathered coast-to-coast to celebrate an ageless all-American automotive icon.

An old favorite gets a new edge. Mustang adopted Ford's crisp-lined "New Edge Design" theme for 1999, which nicely updated the basic five-year-old SN95 shape. Front fog lights and larger wheels mark the convertible (right) as a GT. A V-6 coupe brings up the rear, but remained the top-selling model in the line.

Details, details. All 1999 Mustangs were considered 35th Anniversary editions, but special front-fender emblems were affixed only to base and GT models, not SVT's Cobras. Some 5000 of the GTs left the factory with a celebratory 35th Anniversary package that delivered specific wheels and trim for $2695.

Ford designers really sweated details in giving a "New Edge" to the old SN95 body. But they also aimed for a "retro" air, evident in the return of upright tail-lamps and a prominent C-shape bodyside line terminating in a nonfunctional rear-fender scoop.

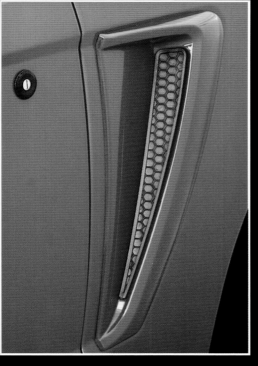

Potent posh. The Mustang's cockpit looked much the same for '99, but added insulation made it easier to hear the more-muscular engine. V-6 horsepower jumped by 40 to 190, while the V-8 tacked on 35 for 250 total.

Snake charms. SVT
Cobra updates for 1999 began
with an exclusive independent
rear suspension (top left), a
first for Mustang. Plus, a V-8
boosted horsepower to 320,
up 15. New white-faced
gauges and special interior
trim were also Cobra-specific.

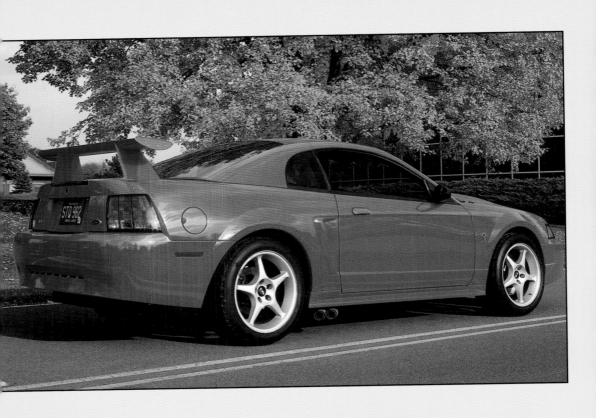

Sensational stand-in. The Cobra was sidelined for 2000 while SVT fixed an engine problem from '99. But in its place came a heroically winged new Cobra R with 385 horses and sub-five-second 0-60-mph sizzle. Just 300 were built, all red coupes.

Victory force. Drag racer John Force and his Mustang funny cars won their 10th class championship in 2000. Master-tuner Jack Roush, meanwhile, continued offering serious performance parts for road and track alike.

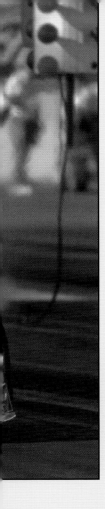

Movie memories. A star turn for 2001 was the GT-based "Bullitt" recalling the hero Mustang fastback of the 1968 Steve McQueen film. Only 6500 were built—all coupes—with many specific features and a starting price of $26,230.

Sales slip. After a strong 1999-2000, sales turned down for two years, perhaps because mainstream models didn't change much. At least Mustang would survive past '02. Its two old General Motors foes didn't. Meantime, the Cobra had resumed production with all 320 advertised horses solidly in the corral.

the 2003 MUSTANG mach 1

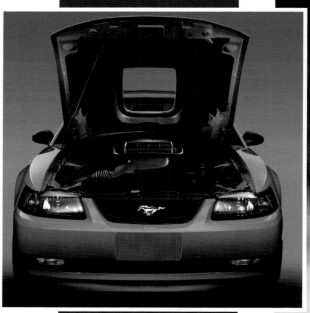

Mach 1 more time. Fo[...]
card by reviving the Mach 1 na[...]
2003 coupe. A genuine "shaker[...]
'69—helped give it 300 rousing[...]

...ved another nostalgia

...a special GT-based

...scoop—shades of

...s. Base price: $28,370

SVT blows it.

The hottest factory Mustang yet bowed for 2003 with newly supercharged SVT Cobras. The "blower" swelled horsepower to 390 and shrunk 0-60 mph to as little as 4.5 seconds. Prices started from $33,460.

Happy 100th for the house that Henry built.

Ford Motor Company turned a century young in 2003, and staged gala celebrations all year long. Among the quieter observances was a limited-edition Centennial Package for Mustang GTs (right). That year's V-6 models offered a new Pony Appearance Package that bundled most GT styling features with Bullitt-type five-spoke wheels, all for a modest $595. As usual, V-6s outsold the V-8 GTs.

Another birthday?

Mustang marked its 40th year in 2004 with a modest $895 Anniversary Package (above) and optional eye-bending "Mystichrome" paint for Cobras (right). An '04 ragtop was Ford Motor's 300-millionth vehicle.

CHAPTER 12

2005

A brand-new breed apart. It hardly seemed possible to some, but Mustang was reborn for 2005 with a road-to-roof redesign—the most complete transformation in the pony-car's fabled history. The result was an appealing blend of nostalgic styling and state-of-the-art engineering.

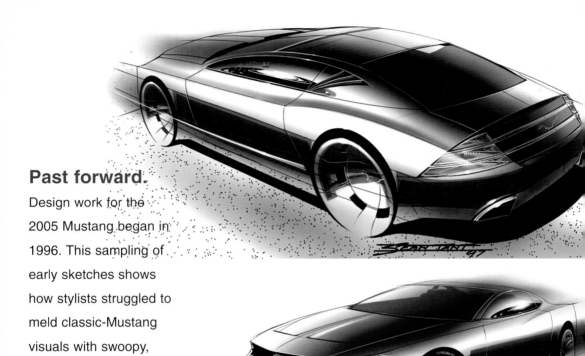

Past forward.

Design work for the 2005 Mustang began in 1996. This sampling of early sketches shows how stylists struggled to meld classic-Mustang visuals with swoopy, futuristic forms to convey an aggressive, new high-performance look.

Icon candy. The 2005 Mustang began to emerge in April 2000 as project S197, but designers kept on exploring and refining ideas into November (opposite page). All of these clay models show a basic look that would survive to the showroom. But devilish details were endlessly debated—especially side-window treatments, tail forms, and front-end appearance.

Historic inspiration. Project S197 was much further along by March 2001. Early dashboard design sought a modern take on the classic "gullwing" panel of 1967-68 Mustangs.

Place in the sun. Car designers insist on checking their work in the light of day to see if it looks as good as it did in the studio. The S197 Mustang faced this acid test—and a few of its predecessors—in spring 2001. Save a few details, it got a big thumbs-up.

Showtime! Ford all but confirmed rumors of an all-new Mustang by displaying this concept coupe and convertible at major 2003 auto shows. Both were exaggerated previews of the upcoming 2005 model—and major hits with the public.

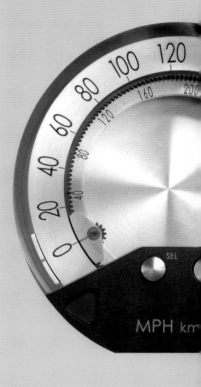

The real thing? Design chief J Mays was pleased with crowd reaction to the 2003 convertible concept. But he wouldn't say how much of the design was locked-in. No wonder. Features like the rear cross-body hoop had already been rejected for production, while other elements were strictly show-car fantasy.

The newest Mustang ever. S197 was the first Mustang having no structural kinship to an existing Ford Motor Company car. Chief engineer Hau Thai-Tang made it plenty strong to handle a new 202-hp V-6—Mustang's most potent base engine ever—and a new 300-horse V-8 for GT models.

Trial by fire—and ice. S197 development cars were put through some 6000 different tests. Among them were cold-weather runs in Sweden, where drivers couldn't resist doing a few smoky burnouts.

Mustang mania strikes again! The 2005 Mustang launched only as a coupe. It was priced from under $20,000 for the base V-6 version, and from around $25K for the hot GT (above). Ford couldn't build them fast enough. New features included dashboard lighting that could be changed from green to one of 125 other hues.

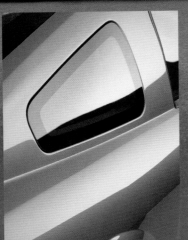

Cool class. All '05 Mustangs looked like a million—even low-cost base V-6 coupes like this one. Critics and customers alike loved the retro styling cues inside and out. Yet, Mustang had a youthful freshness all its own.

Ragtop renaissance.

New base and GT convertibles bowed in early 2005. Careful engineering kept the weight penalty to just 175 pounds, yet they were easily the tightest, quietest Mustang droptops ever.

Snake's alive! Due for 2007 is the hot new Shelby Cobra GT500 coupe. Aggressive styling features are fully matched by a supercharged V-8 with some 450 hp. Shades of the 1960s!

Ride on! What's next for Mustang? Hard to say, but it's bound to be exciting. After 40 years, the original ponycar is still with us—and going stronger than ever.